LIZZIE, SPEAK

LIZZIE, SPEAK

POEMS BY KAILEY †EDESCO

Lizzie, Speak by Kailey Tedesco

Copyright © 2019, Kailey Tedesco

All Rights Reserved.
Printed in the United States of America.

Cover Photo: Kailey Tedesco, Emily Tedesco, Zach Tedesco
Editors: Courtney Leigh Jameson & KT Gutting

First Edition Book
978-1-7323992-3-5

Published by White Stag Publishing LLC
www.whitestagpublishing.com

I don't know what I have said. I have answered so many questions and I am so confused. I don't know one thing from another. I am telling you just as nearly as I know. - Lizzie Borden

†

For Lizzie Borden's Neighbor
& My Great-Great-Grandmother,
Elsie Hawcroft

INNARDS

II.   LIZZIE, WHAT HAVE WE DONE?

LIZZIE, SPEAK

lizzie,   you're home now   with the replica davenport in the parlor
portraits of andrew & abby   faces with black   holes rimming their wounds

lizzie, you own places of last breath   skulls as mantelpiece trinkets   eggs benedict

come morning   where bridget   crouched to mop vomit

lizzie, your parents   reduced to carpet stain   i scavenge for you
monomaniacally   find your words   forming the weather

hill people lining my bodice in red churches the color
of morphine tour of europe inside my beheaded pigeons
never my real mother second sister missing eyelids
never in want of a husband the noise of sex
slouching from their doorway into my own

lizzie, you found me   i felt you pull my ankles   drag me from bed
your voice   a fungal infection   bursting through rug   what is left to say

lizzie, with axe   with hatchet   with hand fan
depicting a scene of the eifle tower

lizzie, naked   dressed only in shadows   from blinds   blood
down both legs   bad memory   loving daughter   kept in my locket

lizzie, a b&b housecat   miserable lilac lining the plaque   all suffocating unknowingly
on the bloodspill   in question   i father-son-holy spirit my forehead

lizzie, fit your eyes   into my sockets

come, speak   what you have done

LIZZIE, COME FORTH

CLAIRVOYANCE

stitched wounds
fruit-bruise &
the bodies

of parents overnight
the dining table.
i once ate a bowl

of porridge
raisin-lit between
my father's knees.

his belly-wound
star-gaped
& licked

a fortune lipped
with beeswax
vaseline

breaths
like anemones.
my supper danced

exotic & i exorcized
my clothing
kimono-stroked

my shoulders
let velvet bend
spirits from

the blood
make witch cakes.
this midwifery

harvesting ghosts
from the holes
that caused them

has left me
open
for too long

THEY SAY LIZZIE KEPT STUFFED GHOST-HEADS ABOVE HER SOFA

flies are always divining
mycology from morning
coffee

godawful.

the people of the hill say
they saw
her nose

turn at the scent
of bergamot down
step-mother's leg

o' mutton.
they say
every killer-

girl has a music box
heart: wound up &

spinning, numbering
its loves
penumbral-ly

until it doesn't
pirouette any
longer & it is hungry

for more braids
to ribbon down
the banisters

LIZZIE, COME BACK

no place like home has its lights out. someone who lives there brags about sleeping through anything. warm milk & ceiling fans hypnotize me pregnant with white horses hoofing my gut. it's kantian: some one will always die if it isn't me first, or else killers come bombing & i rest safe with jade stain circling my finger. stop dragging me from hell. i'm absolutely covered in panoply. the stars embroider me in soap bubbles & the stars choose me, but i will never growl when you need me to. you kill me uphill   & it hurts / it hurts / it hurts

HERE, I APPROACH OAK GROVE CEMETERY

in the bath   my wetness ladles   outwards
dresses me couture   i am always nursing

this little imaginary   zodiac
my body arcs   a bell tower   & i am afraid

of the ghosts that live up there – maggots
for the people   who voice me   a bad choir of changelings

so unwanted   will they even remember   my favorite cheeses
once i change   to dead? to feel the crossover – evaporate

in plums, tumble through a land of arson – my own hair
caramelized & lapped up

doesn't this moonlit theater   cemetery matinee   make my eyes glow hypnotizing?
aren't i the star of your midnight feature   a scarlet herring? the rain

always comes   misting my wrists   glitchy
i am dying   out   an obliteration stage-left

in the foreground   vhs tape with the ribbon
ripped out   all fuzz in the pause

i am every stressed   out pine tree   drowning
out the static   of the tv   left playing –

make this room choke   on my echo   i am so afraid
everyone i love   will never be   a ghost

this sorry earth begs   us towards
the appalachians – find swedenborg   find

sea fingers   find salty chenille & kiss it all
with lots of tongue   this is an ending

you won't want to miss

WITHIN THE HOUSE WITH NO HALLWAYS

mother always measured evil in murder-eyes
skull-haunting   broadcast-news unfocused & staring

downwards all at once   every stuffed lion wants me
to join their cult & i am   seriously considering it

amethyst the shape of my body   clobbered
my toenail bright indigo   like we were dancing bad on shag rugs

& i pretend-yelled *there's a stag in here!* but   the music
the music!   my tea-dyed night   gown   starched from falling

lightly down stairways   always with my neck   oscillating cherry
gloss in my hair   my body has been excavated & my organs

labeled in marmalade recyclables   i'm diorama-built   still pretty
though   body death-gentle like broken eyeglass

housekeepers come often   for my red-streak touch up
blood numbered   to represent my place   in archeology

PSYCHOMETRY I

back barn, wooded over & zapper-lit. a piece of top-skull, curved. a tiny moon or enlarged fingernail. hands placed around it. finger bones feeling the hollow of their ancestor. hair still mossed to the head. stubborn against plucking. a prayer. & then another prayer. & then a question. *to what lock does she belong?* in the after of a death, the mess keeps chosen pronouns. an identity in itself. something to feed. tea sloshes around the bowl & the aftertaste of calcium & dust shows us forwards

SUPERNATURAL ELOQUENCE

this will be a ritual tomorrow   i put on my mourning
beads. i've had tea in the lyceum

my words / their words / our words /
froggy voiced the dummy on my wrist. i'm a woman filled

& they make believe my fill is not of
woman. my father's exact words were:

your caul was like the inside
of a pumpkin & this must mean he believed

my mother was the pumpkin outside.
they think my language is plasm.

they think my body is a jewelry box.
there are a thousand single hairs inside me

none of them my own
clinging on gold brooch / tie clip / lachrymatory bottle

but i promise none of them
will volunteer to do the talking

LIZZIE LIKED THE CIRCUS AS A GIRL

you *must* break every bone
                    feed them

to a neighbor / a tiger / a step-child
            look here

a water lily in my lung
fevering my dreams

two poppets chasing me with pocket-watch foreheads

it's time i buoyed
from leaping waters with my picnic

braids in skull-moss
you must frame me when i'm finished

let them paw around   my innards
let them pull   ripe orchards   from my gut

            all pear blossom & pigeons

oh, grand-jury   call me oedipus / elektra
call me safe

banishing wraiths   with glitter
            twigs behind the house   my heart still

            a plunking midway organ
it bangs out

a village of jump-rope   curses
            all in good fun / fat pockets

RECIPE FOR ECTOPLASM

let me make you a poultice   wet cheesecloth / flour-paste / honey
for sweetness &   *ABRACADABRA*

wadded at the threshold of my gag reflex   my sister once sat me down
to teach me a talent but i pretended i could not snap

my fingers   could not tip the table no matter
my practice   let me remind you   my throat is a lozenge

of your relatives with velvet umbrellas   rosary-bound wrists
here in my body   a telephone   of rapped tables   every word

you've never heard blooms   from my airways in a grand hock
bile delivering salt prints   on conveyors   i use my cuff to wipe sour

milk & shout in my own dialect about the murder
& how it never lived a day   inside my bedroom

i say i am your hypostases   lace-dressed & drunk   on alphabets
death draws on me but in no timeline   i remember

I AM A CASTLE / I AM A BRIDE

i am so dangerous
in my tight

whalebone

water moats my veins
like electric & i am

turning infrared   i am
smiling so whitely

through your tesla radio
all teeth

every one of you
cries me

so far i might as well
be falling

all of you
dress me in chills

of cold fingernails
& buttoned scolioses

i am a stairway
of caskets torchlit

& waiting
for the largo

of my own thrumming
hands to pull

at an arcana
i cannot remember

MY BODY, BRIMMING

i have tossed laser-cut stars
against velvet curtains

as though i am
a sudden force of nature stirring

astrology as easily as swirling
a glass of red wine

i was kept
behind arched doorways
as a child

left to the company
of acrylic madonnas
who whispered names

of everyone
on earth
i would never know

to pray for
until it was
much too late

i name the children
within me
long before

they're due
to sleepwalk
my marrow

& i try to welcome
their attempts
at clawing

LIZZIE PORTAL / LIZZIE VIRGIL

let me thread you, small bloodlet

every breathing body is absolutely smeared with rubies,

tangled strands from beneath the skin

i cross my heart

i've never thieved in my life

let me show you where i was

bed-dreaming

avoiding the hall-sick

gluing the heads back to my dear birdies, laughing

& laughing

as they flapped through my skirts

LEGERDEMAIN

little girls under the age of 12 can teach their muscles to be ghosts. lift & drop a foot without leaving the ground. snap a finger backwards from within the skin. mother's daughter used to tell us to be quiet. locked the door & said *someone is in the house*. i heard noises. pots & pans falling down stairwells. gasps like kettles. she returns. a bird on her wrist, biting at her fingers. biting & biting as she strokes its head. she says   *no one is here*   *but us*

LIZZIE NEW AGE / LIZZIE NEW WAVE

goat-milk butters my dialect
heartfelt   i am lounging on plum-sward

& these waves thieve my shoes   something about this ghost
has gone carte de visite   & i keep on living

to lop off my hair   how often can i scry myself
a mouth full of sugar

papa denies me a new   set of pens   i dare him to breakfast
my slipping   unconscious

slurp kipper memories   drop questions for god
i'll go on cobwebbing the walls   with my echo

let these orbed photos corner
my name   the victrola glitters the hem

of my dress   i am posing post-mortem
& braceleting mother's   cold wrist

i am wishing to tell you something innocent

you've mortared the looking glass

        your mind is made up

LIZZIE ROMANTIC / LIZZIE RHEUMATIC

there i go fainting
down the marbled grand staircase

one hand on my forehead, palm-
upwards

somewhere a god
wears a cameo of love lines

somewhere closer a storm
brews my colicky gut

i am all nerves
in my nightgown of marrow

dearest dental cavity
won't you balance this vase

on your crown
while i recite my alibi

constable constellate
my pores & leave me

salt-browed & quite beholden
this jury swears

so help me
that seawater puppeteers

my reproductive organs
imagine the sirens

pulling my ovaries by string
don't mind me

costuming
this hysterectomy

luxe in my thigh gap
i'll get off

even with cudgel-blood
rouging my jowls

I AM LOST / I AM CURSED

the truth is

i sit here at this table alone

the truth

is i can hold

no hands to invoke

yet here

a cast of ballerinas

casting shadows gentle as dust

sill-settling the blood across

satin chests

show me what i need

to see

dancers pile against me

fluttering at my ribcage

sperm desperate

to osmose a membrane

one specter is tendu beside

my wilting cardio-cavity

LIZZIE IS TRAPPED IN A WOMAN IN PERIL PICTURE

the smell of a harp, purpling   & enter me

all dressed in black black black / with silver
buttons & a choker of ghost-teeth all dead-ankle

asleep. i want to wake. god, i want to wake up
but your glossy aura is kissing the brains

out of my ventricles – it makes me sick & what color
was the blood? / *red, blue, yellow, green?*

what technicolor odor is this? what color is the way
i've been sleep-locking

doorways? what color
is bloody mary / bloody

m*ary* gushing your own name
back & back like a tree-swing?

i am only pretending to sleep now. i've learned
to slow my breathing. touch me

like a spirit board & feel my hands
possessed by barren ovaries, possessed by

the curling auguries
in my tea, possessed by the guff

of my own caesarian
crawling

            crawling

APPORT

a beast by the road dies bone-joint

by bone-joint – mighty knees

made holograms thirsting

for blood. an entire mink

drools from my lips

in the wick-light – the secret

is swallowing

everything that's touched

my vulva erects

a garden shadowed

by winter – ancient statues

crumb down my thighs

all you have lost prevents me

from nudity   i menstruate

gold leaf in the name

of everything holy   i open

my legs for every sweet

of your childhood

mangos & peppermints

& raspberry aspic

to crown

all at once

LIZZIE, WHAT HAVE WE DONE?

LIZZIE/ LIZBETH

I.

a drowned infant returns
to me veiled in amniotic fluid –

she is winged / whiskered / buttered
with the grease of afterlife.

i hold the small daughter
who is only my daughter

for now. i let
her charge my palms,

make my body
smell of salt.

she speaks to me
in the language of channeling

II.

my daughter's mother
left her & now

she is my mother, too. i let
her nurse, whiskers to me

& from her strength
a wilderness

of disentombment. my nose
is an exit for those

who have lost their tongues,
for those whose bodies

soak in the gems
of mud

III.

speech is a sneeze of existence

i drape ghost juice across me like large furs

& i've never felt more beautiful.

my daughter taught me to wire the frozen river

& shout *is anyone out there alive?*

she gave me two glass eyes

irised with bloodstone

so i can see when a body still

has its orbiting moons

LEVITATE

my teeth lift first   crack
with lipstick   my soul slides   from my body

a matchbox   i stand
dressed in bell sleeves   on my childhood porch

my mother calls to me   & a cone
of ocean siphons me upwards   voice first.

i am a bar of soap   this instant
    shell-shaped   so prone to foaming

    over   my blood-glimmer spills
    equations on my arm

physical mediums   are real & my wide
    open mouth chokes

on imaginary numbers   my father
    is back

    he says he's forgotten   his ring
on the kitchen sink

he says to remember

    lizzie who took the stairs
    after her burial   soiled her

childhood bed   it is here i understand
    the finality of leaving

BLACK VELVETY / SILVER FEATHERY

i strangling have kept pets
spiders / bees / turkey vultures

all cramped inside my shredded
nylons   made roomy

in me, bestiaries lush
emerald as fungus

in me, a wide rainforest splays
& the wings fuzz

in my throat   ghosts go to me
when they die

i cage
them like rosary

hear the cadence of possession
swarm my innards   all these creatures

damned to eternities
grafted from my body's

              starving

DIVINE ATTRIBUTES PROVEN THROUGH MEDIUMSHIP

i toss my bread-crusts out the window. slats feed me bars of sunlight, cocoa-dusted in evening. my pillows teach me how to resurrect. pink satin, synthetic. flower petals square-jawed at the bordering. a bottle of stolen perfume, lavender & myrrh. candles unlit & no fire escape. this is a sanctuary, i think, laying backwards to the pillows. how pregnant will i be when this is over? i pinch at my nipples testing for milk. in three years i will have seen death as many times. kiss at least one body on the cheek while searching for a wick at the uvula. i pray for the return of her lips, bursted on impact. by her, i mean both the one that died & the death itself

I REMAIN UNFORGIVEN ON THIS SIDE OF THE VEIL

i lay awake often wondering when i will do
the most terrible thing i will ever do?

how will my body react to that possession & is possession
only an excuse? will my body be worse

when filled with only the echo
of my body? my mother with lipstick-blotted eggs

tells me to keep ouija away, to swallow
necromancy like a handcuff key & distill my blood's wandering

sleep will never come easily again
i will need to set

an altar in my airways
brandish sage with my teeth

ROSABELLE / UNRELIABLE

i am obsessed with no ghost & no body
rests in my body

sit hunchbacked across the table
& remind your shoulders to hyperventilate

a greasy dream   my morphine
muffs our wrists in approval

my spirit-lips clasp the tourniquet
of thawed fingers   ringed

ruby & tiger jaw & moonstone & silver
ringed at the neck with half-moons

branding white nighties chantilly
i salivate for a body emerging

furred with the smoke of carnage
i coax a certain ambergris

to inhabit my soul-box & airways
to speak the language of saints

protected   my netherworld has offed itself
in a bed of cotton   the room

is coughing up rose gold   whetting
each sheet to a shroud of soured

lilies   still milking

LIZZIE'S LOST MOTHER / LIZZIE'S LOST SISTER

it's a rush to connect with a spirit. one house
with brick walls & one house with green
paint. some floors ashen /
must-wet / powdered

in doughnuts we licked
from our palms. i need to keep your
aural clippings / cigarette
dust / lavender

placenta. you kept uteri & a baby
ghost-born. i'm that baby's
daughter & i've no ear
for tongues.

i hear an orphan /
barren / suckling light. i hear
bad static & cpr-ed
pear seeds, attempts

to connect. i bury your music
boxes, the ones i'd wind
all at once. 100 ballets
haloing my detachment. you could see

meals through my opacity: biscuit
heart / corn lung / gravy appendices –
i'm eating. now come find
my skeleton teeth.

i'm bleeding

PSYCHOMETRY II

you have old poppets
in your attic

their tiny mouths
hinge slack-jawed & nectar

sweet dusts
(this is a small secret)

i will sugar-douse
my corsets

each morning
the cats mirror their

dregs   cloy
the tulips over-splattered

stop your thieving
& postmark my ouija

back to me
keep the planchette

passive
i am trying to

look lovely these days
i eat creme-stuffed

pastries & scrub-
meat-confetti

raw from
my dress

LIZZIE INGENUE / LIZZIE PSYCHO-BIDDY

my wig-stand has spoken
a necromancy
& i am the demon covered

in ocean-water   thick
chiffon waves dousing
for a small green house

with no hallway
i make these beds
again & again & again

wait for the hatchet to   storm her
i *know* the hatchet will
storm her the wild

blood stampedes
the velveteen   violet-ing
the color   all the danger

drools from me
like chandeliers
pearls & opals

three strands thick
crescent-ing my body
i am on a stage of bedding

alone with my dust
lunacy encores
i stay up

singing softly
to myself

BENT SPOON

these iron maiden trees
smear the lake
make my ankles weak

i love painting my fingernails   with honey
& licking them new

&   once   a witch burned
on that tree above my head

i cried without my teeth

the door bell of the wilting
house is too compelling

limbs of morphine tangle
my braids & they belong

to the ghost   lizzie

come play in all this toile-green water

            i scream

put on your black gown
& wake up floral-lipped

                far passed this dressing screen of stars

MAKE ME SPINDLY

come upon these briars carpeted
pinkly & drench yourself in small

cuts, puncture wounds, violet
fruits. so much of what you desire

is made from your own body. speak
of your cloak & pillow. speak in

sobs of gold leaf – currency to burn
cheeks like hot ovens of butter

bread & mutton. come see me
for shifting palms & fingerprints,

life lines centipedal. my breath
is the only kingdom. come to my

sternum antlered in brown
moss / valerian bloom, hung limp

to the wall. pull at the threads
of your augury, knife-cut to knife-

cut, blood spill against skin, against
bark, against seed. needles pile

to frozen roses – here i lay varicose
in the winter of your eye

THE LIGHTS ARE WARM & COLORED

after William Norfolk

when every little bone
of my body
has calmed, when

october, when the sky
gallops / trapezes / gulps
when the fortune teller

removes her rings, ascends
i have died at that time
without knowing

& only small
flashes of light
against the stucco

ceiling & inside my
closed eyes
show me the backyards

long prickled

sheets have frosted
around me, shrines
of southern fruit

orange / peach / nectarine
all contused juices & aroused
with insects —

i sit at the kitchen table
asking for candy apples
wedge-sliced

while my sister
ignores me in favor
of god —

the earth of this moment
whirlpools & lakes
my blood still

LIZZIE'S SISTER / THE BASEMENT

the sisters i'm thinking of light candles
          on their molars – waxy moonlight,
artificial. we have taught them to
          hold the hands

of strangers at a young age. they have learned
          to pull the bones of hand from skin
of hand making empty palms
          as offerings.

the tin bowl is kept
          between floorboards, full
of sticky dimes, full of paper cranes – full. these girls
          talk of death like they know it,

like they've always been full of it. deer
          mice flee from beneath
their fingernails making mother
          beat their wrists like rugs

scrubbing skin hot & then
          gone. these girls have soap
in their mouths. it's stolen.

tastes yellow
          but not lemon. someone
sleeps on their carpet at night. they've licked

          it cat-dry. these girls use eye-
lashes to auger, nose to floor,
          sipping the maple

WE ARE TURNING GOLD / WE ARE DYING

what i'm saying
is a lie

you brought a guillotine

to my bedroom
& told me

a long story about a girl
murdered by a cistern

inhuman   i asked
if it was the cistern

or the girl that
was not human & you

looked   quiet

this lie feeds me
spoonfuls of latent images

each slowing a grove of stumps
bare headed & blank palmed

i looked up
& through the dead trees

i saw violet light
chipped like toenails

what i'm saying is still

a lie

PRE-CODE SPIRITUALISM

i cannot work-a-bone   until i've undressed
        this ghost-froth   from my membrane

i am all leeched with auras   cast-off & veil-clung
        tell it to me straight & do not censor my fortune

whisper from your deathbox   switch my body red
        with electric & sift through the star-ash   threading me gold-blooded

munchausen swallows me up   with all these rabbits & i bear
        the migraine of their demonic possession

i do knuckle-magic under the table   you swore
        you'd return with a grimoire of matinees for my quick-

drying eyeballs   i want to have that vision we talked about
        i'm sitting in this empty   waiting for you & your thought

 dust to come party-streaming from my blouse-sleeves & collar
        i promise i won't be afraid this time   i know how to convince myself

that the negative of your shape is   a light
        i can remember

I ASK THE NETHERWORLD IF LIZZIE DID IT

I: spirit board:

i d-o-n-t
t-h-i-n-k
i-t-s
g-o-i-n-g
t-h-e
w-a-y
y-o-u
w-a-n-t
l-i-z-z-i-e
i-s
t-h-e
o-n-l-y
p-e-r-s-o-n
t-h-at
c-a-n
g-e-t
y-o-u
t-h-r-o-u-g-h
t-h-e
w-a-y

II. eight of wands

just see
those staffs through the kitchen sink
or a little bit of
coffee   things are not okay
but it's not too much
for you to eat

III. iOS X predictive:

lizzie borden hurt my face
& now i feel better

i think it's a bad thing
but that's what happened last night

so i'm going to call her tomorrow

face the way of your life
& then
i'll be there

LIZZIE'S PIGEONS / LIZZIE'S AXE

on the morning of my heart's bursting
the squabs' wings dismember
in my hair   it is here that i shrieked

my eyes backwards   stretched my arms
to the crown molding   let my breath
suffocate

the room   this glass shatter
reds the walls in starbursts   laughs
a horoscope of their final

moment   my socks should
be of no concern to you, father   please remove
            yourself

from my ear   what is the word
for being *not* with child? i wear a scarf to
keep

myself my own   a dial tone eats up
the family   now, it is just
            you & i

MILK BELLY

in a dream
i buy myself white
oleanders / death

cups / potassium
cyanide – i can
only awaken

once a year
& even then
it is a burden

to lift eyelids
from within.
small me

in a modest
dress, boston-
stolen, tumors

each rib before
reaching the eye.

when i hinge the lid
closed your body

will be my body
& your tongue

will taste the milk
of strangers

IN WHICH I ATTEMPT TO EXORCISE LIZZIE FROM ME

i understand you best when i am you
        on a stage with suellen vance as nance o'neil

so many degrees   removed from my body
      your warmth   no longer mine   your thoughts

no longer heaving   feathers in my hair
      the number of times the hatchet brazed your kin

is still a wonder to me   on sweet mornings
      i am in your bedroom   waking   to scones

my body asleep in yours   your body asleep in mine
         each other's mothers

on other mornings i expect to find the lip
      of axe cutting into my own face

blood smearing my pillow   dried brown
from years of sitting   my great great grandmother

your neighbor   a child   sang your poem
      before anyone, maybe   & you found me in that rhyme

i refuse to play you any longer   your chilled bones
      around my ankles   hurt me in new ways

i find myself again   in your green house
      not a single living thing except me

& the songs i wish to play   on the radio
      two dollar styrofoam coffees   down the street

that belong to my ritual   alone
      what happened that day   i didn't know

i need every piece of you   to leave me
      burn the evidence in the sink

BLACK MOOD / MAPLECROFT

today is the day i become
a girl of swans, not

pigeons, not prussic
acid

i buy the lamps
of silk-screen & beads

with the coins i always wanted
stop telling me what i already know

stop your sistering & plucking
at my roses like a bad neighbor

i shake the shadow
from me   i shake your entire

nuptial arrangement
i wear my parasol

like a third arm even
when the river sweats

the pathway ugly   i do
not care how you know

my name only that you
do & i never ever had to

tell you   this is your airway
& my only version

of the truth   now come

hear the meat inside me

ACKNOWLEDGEMENTS

The author would like to wholeheartedly thank the following journals for featuring these poems, sometimes under a different title or in an earlier form.

Charles River Journal: "they say lizzie kept stuffed ghost heads above her sofa" and "lizzie is trapped in a woman in peril picture"

Muse/A Journal: "rosabelle / unreliable" and "pre-code spiritualism"

Grimoire: "recipe for ectoplasm"

Boston Accent Lit: "lizzie, speak"

TL;DR: "lizzie portal / lizzie virgil" and "lizzie's pigeons / lizzie's axe"

Mystic Blue Review: "make me spindly" "the lights are warm & colored" "supernatural eloquence" and "milk belly"

Always Crashing: "levitate"

Glass: A Journal of Poetry: "lizzie's lost mother / lizzie's lost sister"

Blue Fifth Review: "lizzie, come back"

Nice Cage: "black velvety / silver feathery"

Sea Foam Mag: "psychometry I"

Phoebe Journal: "lizzie romantic / lizzie rheumatic"

Anti-Heroin Chic: "clairvoyance" and "legerdemain"

Ovunque Siamo: "my body, brimming"

Moonchild Magazine: "i am a castle / i am a bride"

OCCULUM: "we are turning gold / we are dying"

Bone Bouquet Journal: "here, i approach oak grove cemetery" and "lizzie new age / lizzie new wave"

FLAPPERHOUSE: "i ask the netherworld if lizzie borden did it"

glitterMOB: "lizzie liked the circus as a girl"

Wyrd & Wyse: "black mood / maplecroft"

I would also like to thank my mom for teaching me the Lizzie Borden rhyme as a child, both of my parents for allowing us to skip school so we could visit Lizzie Borden's house, Electric Literature for publishing my essay on Shirley Jackson & Lizzie Borden (which in many ways was the spark that ignited this project), Joey Edsall and Emily Tedesco for watching numerous Lizzie documentaries and ghost hunts with me, and the Lifetime Movie Network for reminding me that Lizzie's story is far from finished.

†

Farewell, Lizzie Borden

WHITE STAG

Printed and bound by PG in the USA